THE OLD METAL DESK

God Speaking Through Scratches,
People, and Scripture

Larry Linville

authorHOUSE®

AuthorHouse™
1663 Liberty Drive, Suite 200
Bloomington, IN 47403
www.authorhouse.com
Phone: 1-800-839-8640

First published by AuthorHouse 2/13/2008

Printed in the United States of America
Bloomington, Indiana
This book is printed on acid-free paper.

ISBN: 978-1-4343-6513-2 (sc)

Library of Congress Control Number: 2008900979

Dedication

I could not publish this book without dedicating it to my father, Lawrence Ray Linville. He was the oldest of seven children and the father of seven children. He quit school after the eighth grade to help the family. He was always a loving and giving person.

His generosity was exhibited in the gift of the desk which is pictured on the front cover of the book. My strong emotions looked for expression which I was unable to find until March of 2007. The poem "The Old Metal Desk" was that expression finally surfacing in the form of a poem.

My father died in a truck/train accident in 1965 at the age of 51. This desk has been with me to this day to remind me of his greatness and his love.

Thanks, Dad.

Contents

The Old Metal Desk

He never told me he loved me—at least I don't recall.
He was father to seven kids, and I know he loved us all.
He worked long hours every day—long as he was able
just to put food upon our meager table.
He took us all to church whenever Sunday came
but had to miss, because of work, most every baseball game.
His approval seemed evident when I heard the call of God.
And at my first sermon, he affirmed it with a nod.
He visited our house not long after we were wed.
He glanced into my office, and not a word was said.
I know he saw my makeshift desk—
two orange crates and some wood
And I thought nothing of it as he left and said, "Be good!"
About a week or maybe two, I had some very strange luck.
There was a great big package delivered by a truck.
We cut the tape and pulled the sides apart so we could see
a brand-new metal desk my father sent to me.
Although he couldn't afford it
he bought this for his boy.
And he knew what he had given me was much more than a toy.
The desk is now rusted and broken—
the evidence of years and wear.
It still stands in my house, unused
with "I love you" written everywhere!

Everything Works Out for the Best

"Everything works out for the best."
These words he kept deep in his chest.
When times in our life
were packed full of strife,
he'd say, "Everything works out for the best."

Where did he get these strange words?
Was it something he thought he had heard?
He just found those words great
like Romans eight twenty-eight.
"Everything works out for the best."

"Everything works out for the best."
He often put these words to the test.
He believed they were true
and he'd pass them to you:
"Everything works out for the best."

His life was taken too soon
on that February afternoon.
But his words echoed loud
to that large funeral crowd:
"Everything works out for the best."

His words are still with me today.
They come to my mind when I pray.
My faith has been led
by these words that he said:
"Everything works out for the best."

It Was Just a Dream

Jacob was fleeing from his troubled life behind.
He laid his head on a stone to try to get some rest.
Angels on a ladder to heaven brought God down to earth.
When he awoke and looked around
it was just a dream, but it seemed so real.

My father was at worship in my church
even though he'd been dead for years.
I was serving Communion
which I'd never done for him.
It filled a great, sweet place in my heart.
It was just a dream, but it seemed so real.

Jacob began to consider this thing.
"God was in this place and I knew it not."
His life was so lifted;
he was filled with such joy.
It was just a dream, but it seemed so real.

After the service, we went out to eat.
We talked about all that had happened
since he was taken from me.
The conversation was almost endless, and my joy overflowed.
It was just a dream, but it seemed so real.

If Jacob had rolled over and gone back to sleep,
he'd have missed so much of the courage he needed
to take his long trip.
The time he took to ponder what it meant
helped him look at the world through new eyes.
It was just a dream, but it seemed so real.

I, too, could have ignored what happened that night.
I'd have missed the boosting of my life.
I might have simply filed it away
with the simple words, "That was strange!"
It was just a dream, but it seemed so real.

Jacob blessed that stone pillow and named it "God's house."
He went on his way with a special closeness to his God.
My heart has a pillow of that special visit.
It is blessed in my heart even today.
It is also God's house, and it has strengthened me on my way.
It was only a dream, but it seems so real.

Grampy

My Grampy was always a stranger to me.
His vagabond nature made him rare to see.
He and Grammy dropped in once in a while
but they didn't stay long, then they left with a smile.

He was a jack of all trades and master of none
but his stories all claimed he was number one.
A newspaper man without a Pulitzer Prize
but he claimed he had one without blinking his eyes.

With trumpet in hand, he made the great claim
that he invented jazz but never had fame.
He wrote many marches and led many bands
but when his help was needed, he had injured his hands.

When we asked him to prove his great claims about jazz
we said we hadn't heard it, and nobody has.
He said, "You can look it up in the book,"
then walked away with his smug little look.

When he started his stories, we sat back in doubt
with a smile on each questioning face.
We knew he was lying, but he said it so well
as he loudly presented his case.

It finally hit me how he influenced my life.
At first I just took a wild stab.
Now I'm convinced from the depth of my heart
he gave me the great gift of gab.

Pleasant Grove

I began attending Pleasant Grove Church
when we moved close by; I was just four.
Mrs. Miller entertained with a sandbox
and Bible stories she told on the floor.

The basement of that little country church
divided with a curtain on a rod.
Each classroom with the noise from all around—
a special place for us to learn of God.

Mrs. Fryar's class caught my attention
each week I heard as she so loudly said,
"Now, children, what is our motto today?"
Each student repeated each word she led.

Worship in that church drew me close to God
as I learned nothing that was sinister.
And the preacher asked me when I was twelve
If I thought I might be a minister.

After all my training was completed
and I preached in some churches of my own,
I was asked to come preach a revival
in that little church in which I had grown.

The revival had such great attendance.
They came out to hear their own little boy.
We worshipped and heard the Word of God preached
And our hearts were filled with the greatest joy.

A big storm came up after the weekend.
There were showers and lightning all around.
One bolt from the clouds hit the little church
And the building burned clear to the ground.

God's Word must go on, and storms can't stop it.
A beautiful church stands there yet today.
I'm asked by the church to preach there again.
This time we'll pray that the storms stay away.

Always Have a Sermon

A young pastor went to another church
to sit in a pew and observe
an experienced pastor weave a web
of words with much calmness of nerve.

The service began a few minutes late.
Hymns were sung and the prayers were prayed.
Offering plates were passed down all the rows
and a special number was played.

The young preacher sat back to watch and learn
from the pastor's well-prepared speech.
Before getting comfy, he was asked
to come to the pulpit and preach.

He stood to apologize and decline.
"I don't have a sermon," he said.
After he was seated, she preached the Word.
And the gospel was fully spread.

Last "amens" were said when she went to him.
She gave him an important clue.
"Young man," she said, "you need to know
to always have a sermon with you."

First Communion

It was my first Sunday at my new church.
I felt like I was on review.
They watched each action I took that day,
and wanted to see what I'd do.

I stressed as I said my first words so well.
I tried to smile as I spoke.
There's no way I could let the people see
that their new pastor was a joke.

The sermon went well—so far, so good.
Tension had begun to let up.
The prayer of Thanksgiving I had just prayed
and lifted the bread and the cup.

Shot glasses were stacked in trays very high.
I gave to each person who had knelt.
Carefully I placed the tray on the stack;
another good notch in my belt.

Group followed group to the altar to pray.
I was doing it so very well.
My attention left me for just a short time
and trays went flying all to hell.

I wanted to run from the church and hide,
and try to forget this great gaffe.
Their acceptance—a great gift to me.
They taught me it's all right to laugh.

Has-been Preacher

I'm a preacher who's been retired for nearly four long years.
It seems I'm really only known by that big group of my peers.
Things continue well—like they did when I was there.
When the young ones hear my name, they look at me and stare.

I met a young, vibrant preacher that I'd never met before
And we spoke to each other as we stood inside the door.
He told me what his name is and then just what he does.
I said, "I'm just an old has-been who really never was."

If success could be symbolized by a great big wooly beard,
My accomplishments were much less and really kind of weird.
My ministry might more accurately be like some peachy fuzz
I'm just an old has-been who really never was.

I know I did a lot of things that touched some people's life
I joined them in the good times and helped in time of strife.
I've helped young preachers who now are quite a buzz.
So I shouldn't feel like a has-been who really never was.

I think I've been too good at putting myself down.
I may never have ruled the city, but was a big man in my town.
I know I've done the things that some would think are odd
But I guess I'm a has-been who's a still-is to my God.

Sermons about Money

My preaching began when I was quite young
in three little churches while in college.
I was lacking much in experience
And I was also lacking in knowledge.

This eighteen-year-old drove up that first week.
I was early and nervous and afraid.
Quickly, I entered the door of that church
and rapidly to the front, where I prayed.

I practiced my talk alone in that church.
I wanted to be sure it was just right.
With a strong voice and the right chosen words
which I hoped would overcome my deep fright.

The first two persons who entered the door
were the treasurer and his lovely wife.
He was quick to give some advice to me
and it hit me in my gut like a knife.

"We do not preach money from this pulpit,"
were his words, which I can still hear today.
I took a deep breath—I knew I was safe
'cause the sermon was about how to pray.

Many years have come and gone since that day
When I was given this self-serving tip.
I've never preached money—not even once
But I have often preached of stewardship.

The Closet

The sound system was not working.
The microphone clung to each word I said
with the strength of super glue.
The lights were not flashing on the sound board;
a nuclear scientist was not needed to know
electricity was lacking.
A breaker switch in a small room
controlled the current flow.
But who could do this simple task?
Who could I call to flip the switch?
My wife was standing near that door
with two acolytes in place
poised to light the altar candles.
She knew all about the switch.
The worship service was in paralysis.
Everything was stopped.
Without throwing that switch, we could not go.
With the greatest of authority
and the meekness as her mate,
I posed a question to my bride
in the strangest set of words.
The question was poorly asked—
the words came out all wrong.
The congregation sat and laughed
and then they laughed some more.
I thought they'd never stop
as I stood red-faced
following my famous words,
"Thelma, could you turn me on—
in the closet?"

Small Boy at a Funeral

I sat in a funeral home today
with an open casket of somber gray.
A four-year-old boy walked up to look in,
with the casket the same height as his chin.

His curiosity seemed to prevail
as he stared at the body in detail.
What were his thoughts as he stood and stared?
I'd like to have asked, but I never dared.

How could his young mind ever understand
something that mystifies the wisest man?
You can't explain it to him, nor can I.
Can you tell a child what it means to die?

His bright eyes were wide open as he turned.
To know all his thoughts, my mind never learned.
Then I was told the deceased was his dad.
My heart became heavy—this was so sad.

It seemed there were no right words I could say.
I opened my heart and began to pray.
I pray that he'll be surrounded with love
from family and friends and our God above.

Anointing Jesus's Feet

O Mary, when you anointed the feet of our Lord
and you used your hair to dry them well,
the fragrance of that costly perfume
gave the room a beautiful smell.

Did you want us to know when you shared your love
that we, too, can let our devotion show?
When we give of our best to our Lord
the aroma gives off a sweet glow.

Judas, do you judge that such acts are a waste?
Should we think more about the poor?
May it be that our acts of sweet love
may help lift them from the floor?

What did you mean, our blessed Lord
when you said the poor would always be here?
Were you really telling that disciple of yours
that his complaining was not so sincere?

Mary's great service of Jesus brought joy.
It should cause each of us to think.
Is our work in the kingdom producing sweet smells
or, like Judas, do we just raise a stink?

Do You Ever Cry Anymore, Jesus

Do you ever cry anymore, Jesus?
You wept over Jerusalem.
Do you cry when you see us today?
We who call ourselves after your name
and think you only hear us pray?
We aren't very loving in the things that we say.
Judging others for what they do—
then condemn them publicly
and claim it's for you.
Do you ever cry anymore, Jesus?

Do you cry when you see us sift through your Word,
when we spit out the gnat of your love
while we swallow the camel of deception?
We throw away someone who is different so quick
without finding out what's making them tick.
Do you ever cry anymore, Jesus?

Do you cry when we search for that one little verse
that supports what fits in our plans,
rather than finding the one
that gives us a glimpse of what you desire?
Do you ever cry anymore, Jesus?

Do those hot tears flow down your cheeks, Jesus,
when you see us use hatred and fear
to influence others to fight our fights
and finance our battles
and echo our slogans?

Do you ever cry anymore, Jesus?

Elijah and the Widow

(based on I Kings 17:8-16)

Her life was nearly over as she gathered firewood.
With her last grain and oil, she'd make them something good.
In her poverty and hunger, she would lie down to rest;
go to sleep and not wake up—she knew that was the best.

Elijah came along to this woman who was bereft.
"First feed me," he said to her, "then you can eat what's left."
He made a crazy promise, which surely led to doubt.
"After you have fed me, your food will not run out."

Can you believe the faith it took for her to feed him first?
She had given him some water to take away his thirst.
She fed him first and then herself and her little boy.
This selfless act was an opening to the greatest joy.

The grain was not empty and the oil did not fail.
She had all she needed as she walked along life's trail.
Had she ignored the command Elijah made that day,
There'd be no good news to share in any way.

Perhaps our joy is running low as we struggle with our lack.
Would we only learn what we give God is truly given back.
To put God first in all we do is the message of this tale.
Serve God through serving others—and you'll have a loaded pail.

Holy Saturday

They watched him die on Friday
or heard that it had happened
while they were hiding in fear.
Tears and words of dismay
passed between them
all night long.
The sun rose on Saturday.
What were they to do?
Everything they had worked for was gone.
It's a good thing they couldn't travel.
That would have been breaking the Sabbath.
They wanted to be together.
They wanted to be alone.
Being together gave safety in numbers
but what if those soldiers found them in a group?
How could this have happened?
Where was that God he talked about?
Think of the most depressing thing that could happen to you
and then multiply it by one hundred,
then you'll know how bad they felt.
If only they could have expressed it
to help us understand today.
Why was nothing written
on that day in between?
It could have helped us
when we feel that deep emptiness.
Remember—they didn't know,
as torturously as they felt that day,
that the opposite was waiting
with the sunrise.

I Have Seen the Lord

She stood speechless at his tomb.
Her mind was searching what had happened—it was such a whirlwind.
Her life had been empty until she had met him.
He had given a glimpse of promise and hope.
She was able to turn her back on her past.
Her future, which was starting to look great, was destroyed.
That empty grave was reflected by her empty soul.

She had watched as they taunted him
when they slammed that thorny crown on his head.
She saw them drive nails and plant that cross in the ground.
She had stood near the cross with his mother so dear
as they fearfully looked at his pain.
She heard every word that he uttered.
Her heart nearly stopped as he took his last breath
and proclaimed "it is finished"—and then he died.
She held his mother so close in her heart
as both of them hugged as they cried.

The Sabbath is over as she walks to his grave.
She didn't know why she was there.
Maybe she just wanted to be close to him.
She needed to think.
Or maybe it was an expression of care.
She panicked as she saw the missing stone.
She approached as fast as she could.
The empty tomb only increased her own emptiness.
How could she go on from this moment in time?
Not only had he been killed
but insult was added to injury
when someone took off with his body.

As she stood by that open door of despair
her life couldn't sink any lower.

A voice spoke but she didn't hear
the noise of her grief shut out other sounds.
"Why are you weeping?" the voice said again.
Perhaps it's the culprit, she thought.
"If you've taken him, please bring him back!"
And small streams become raging rivers.
It took only one word to awaken her hope.

"Mary."
It's Jesus! How could that be?
She ran to embrace him.
"Please, let me be.
Go tell the disciple that you have seen me."

She ran away faster than she had come to this place.
Her life so different, she made record time.
She invaded the gathering.
She set them in action with her words that seemed foolish.
"I have seen the Lord."

To lives that are empty today,
and feel they could not be lower,
who are defeated and hopeless,
and don't know where to turn,
her words can echo in your heart.
"I have seen the Lord."

The news of Easter has not been spread by proof.
No scientist has given us reason to hope.
The media, no matter how mighty they are,
cannot make this message expand.
Easter has come to us down through the years
as person to person the message is given.

"I have seen the Lord."

Jesus Ascended

Jesus ascended.
The disciples watched.
They kept looking up after he was gone.

Two men in robes
stood by their sides.
"Why do you stand looking up?"

They said to go
to Jerusalem
to worship and to pray.

We are like them.
We stand looking up
when we should be looking ahead.

If they kept looking up
and hadn't prayed
They'd not been ready when the Spirit came.

If we worship
we, too, will be prepared
for our own special Pentecost.

Tabitha, Arise

Tabitha, Arise
open your eyes!
You've had your rest
from doing what is best.

Take these needles and thread
for women who need to be led.
Now that you're alive
you'll help others survive.

The church leaders left them out
but you will help them, no doubt.
You're following Jesus—it is true
we see him working through you.

As ages pass, you're alive today
in the hearts of people as they pray.
As they look around and take heed
to locate people who are in need.

As long as people do as you did
and not keep their lighted candle hid.
Your passion will echo throughout the land
where the serving of others is in demand.

The Duct Tape Bible

He carries a paperback Bible.
It's well used, there's no doubt.
Pages are bent and dog-eared
And it has bookmarks all about.

The outside colors have faded much.
Duct tape holds the cover together.
It appears it's the only Bible for him.
There cannot be any other.

It didn't get this way sitting on the shelf.
It's from preparing for Sunday school.
This has worn it inside and out.
And in its own way, it looks so cool.

What shape is your Bible in today?
Does it on your coffee table stay?
Or is it something you reach for
At the beginning of every day?

Walking on Water

Peter saw it.
The strange, ghostlike image
over the dark waves.
To ease his frightened mind, he shouted,
"Jesus, if that's you, make me walk with you!"
Jesus said, "Come."
And he did.
He wasn't graceful
as he tiptoed the raging sea.
He was doing it
and that's what mattered.
He knew he was good
and he soared with confidence—in himself.
He needed the Master to order him, at first.
But as he progressed,
his pride began to grow.
Now he was doing this thing on his own.
He noticed the winds,
which had been there all along.
But now he was troubled.

"What am I going to do about this?"
He knew he couldn't do it
So he cried out for help.
The lesson for you and me, my friend,
is that it's good to try to imitate the Lord.
When we fail, as we all do,
all is not lost.
It's better to imitate and fail
than never to imitate at all.
It was when he changed his focus to himself
that he began to sink.
Let's jump out of the boat today
and imitate the Lord.
And know that when we look at him
and how he lived
and loved
and shared,
when we try and sink
His hand will lift us up.

We Must Obey God Rather than Humans
Acts 5:27-32

Which side would we have been on
as the Apostles were chastised by the authorities?
It wasn't the government arresting them.
It was the church leaders,
the good guys,
those who represented God.

They thought they had handled it with Jesus dead.
But now his followers were carrying on.
We have to put a stop to this.
Let's nip it in the bud.
Don't let it gain momentum.
We'll lock them up and scare them.
Let them know we mean business.
Make an example of them.

They had to protect God from these misfits.
But they didn't know that God was not impressed
by their dedication to what they called the Truth.
God sent angels to unlock the jail doors.
And the next morning
they were back.
Here's Johnny! — or rather, Here's Peter.

Both sides thought they were serving God.
Those leaders didn't realize
their traditions had become their god.
Obedience is good
but obedience to what
or to whom?

We must, Peter answered,
obey God rather than human authority.
We are witnesses
And so is the Holy Spirit.

Through the ages, the church has stood in this place.
Luther and Calvin and Wesley.
What will happen if they have followers?
Yet today the descendants
Of Luther and Calvin and Wesley
Are upset at others who have come along.
What about James Jones and his Kool-Aid gang?
And David Koresh and Waco crowd?
The radical right and the radical left
The non-denominational denominations?

If we "must obey God"
why do we disagree so much?
Do we witness only to what we believe?
Or do we witness along with the Holy Spirit
Given to all who obey God?

A New Gift

I recently opened a great gift.
Opened at a most surprising time.
Was I to celebrate it and jump for joy?
Or would it vanish quickly—and break
like so many of the favorite gifts in my life?
This gift gave a self-expression
to put down in words
the deepest feelings
that resided in my heart.
Prose has been my most trusty tool
as I have birthed sermons for many long years.
Poetry was just a game for rare fun
and usually began with "Roses are red."
I've tried
yes, the Lord knows I've tried
to find the right words
to get from the depth of my innermost parts
an expression that could say what a sermon never could.
When I look to past writings
I now see a slight hint
that the talent was there all along.
But it took this new gift

to open it up and let it flow.
I no longer sit down with a plain paper sheet
and make myself labor for words.
After opening this gift
I find that the words are there
calling me to find the page
on which they will take final residence.
From my heart to my head
a picture takes flight
and appears in my mind's eye
and forms itself upon the page
as I, filled with awe,
watch to see what God has done
through me.
May each of us,
whether poet or not,
open the gift that God gives
and allow God to reach out to the world
by the way God helps us to live.

Abandonment

I took a drive through the old part of the city
where the run-down houses were not very pretty.
Abandonment is present where beauty once shone.
It turned once-grassy lawns to litter and stone.

These bad conditions did not happen overnight.
One by one, each added to the growing blight.
There are many reasons for this sad condition.
Neglect heads the list that killed this proud tradition.

Buildings are not the only victims of this scene.
Abandonment of people is even more obscene.
Damage to the buildings is obvious to see
but people's poor condition is the vital key.

There are many churches that have abandoned folks.
They are like a pretty wheel with some missing spokes.
Once people's lives soared with hopes and faith so high.
Abandoned by the members, their faith had to die.

A church may have stained-glass windows shining so bright
but the life of many members may be an ugly sight.
Abandonment has built a dangerous façade
and the final blow comes as they abandon God.

Can You Hear Me Now?

He walks across your TV screen
with that nerdy little look.
"Can you hear me now?" he asks.
"Good," he said and then he shook.

After seeing this ad a million times
I began to really hate it.
Then I tried to find a helpful way
for me to relate it.

I wonder, when we go our way
at things we think so dear,
if God would like to talk to us
to see if we can hear?

God has spoken since early times
through prophets and speakers galore.
But many present-day spokesmen
say things we should ignore.

God gave his message in a book
we haven't really read.
We may have perused his words
but not heard what he said.

I wonder how God feels today
as we run on a prowl.
You think he might be shouting
"Can you hear me now?"

Crooked Politics
(based on 1 Kings 21:1-21)

King Ahab wanted a vineyard and was willing to pay.
It was in Naboth's family forever and a day.
Naboth said, "I just can't do that, Sire.
You don't have enough cash to acquire."

Ahab pouted and moped all around the house.
Jezy asked, "In Baal's name, are you a man or a mouse?"
She called a meeting for Naboth to attend
with two of her helpers, she plotted his end.

They trumped up false charges for these guys to bring.
They said he cursed God as well as the king.
The plan was completed as they stoned him right there.
And the king took his vineyard as his answer to prayer.

When we look at what's done in our world today
we can see people who still try to betray.
If you worry when you see this kind of crime,
remember, crooked politics go back a long time.

Don't Lower God

Hey, David, I'm so glad you aren't around.
They're doing some things that would make you frown.
Your psalms are uplifting—give God much praise.
They want to make him their ol' buddy these days.

You knew that God can't be captured in words from off the street,
no matter how many righteous phrases we repeat.
You knew that poetry best expresses the obscure
while the words of science just cannot endure.
You said God was Majestic—much higher than we.
And there's no way to write on paper what we see.
Today we want to lower the level to words of prose
And remove the majestic language that you chose.
Some want to bring the Bible into a science class.
Without it, they believe our children just can't pass.
They call this intrusion "intelligent design,"
believing it will open the door to the Divine.
Their efforts are sincere, their motives are pure
and very well intentioned, to be sure.
The effort brings God down to science and prose
and removes the great glory which from the Psalms flows.

Eden's Forbidden Fruit

It wasn't an apple on that tree
that was a temptation for Eve to see.
I know firsthand what cast its evil spell,
so listen closely and I will start to tell.

I'm driving down the road and there I see
a red oval with a Q and a D.
My car turns in and goes up to the door.
Next thing I know, I'm standing in the store.

I'll get a small cone—that won't do much harm.
The girl behind the counter twists my arm.
I open my mouth and what do I say,
"I'll just have a Peanut Buster Parfait."

It wasn't an apple Eve saw that day.
She was tempted by that sinful parfait.
When she passed it on to dear old Adam,
you can be sure the devil really had 'em.

Harry Potter Inquiry

She entered with her pious look
and sized up the backed-up lines.
One by one she approached
the costumes and the signs.

"You here to buy the Harry Potter book?"
she asked with a very righteous sneer.
"Yes," was the enthusiastic reply
as they expected her to cheer.

She made her way through the long human lines,
asking the question almost with a yell.
With each affirmative answer
she said, "You are going to hell."

Before she was ushered from the store,
a person who had refused to budge
said, "I may see you there, my friend,
because it's also wrong to judge."

I Saw God Decorate a Christmas Tree

A scrawny cedar stood all alone
in a pasture on a December morn.
It was more brown than green.
An object that we all would scorn.

One by one the snowflakes fell
from the gray winter skies
and the tree took on beauty
right before my very eyes.

The flakes took their special place
like they were placed with gentle care
because no human being
would know to put them there.

When I came back down that country road,
what beauty was there to see.
The ugly tree had a special aura.
I saw God decorate a Christmas tree.

Jesus Cheer

The cheer began …
"We love Jesus, yes we do.
We love Jesus, how about you?"
A group across the way echoed,
"We love Jesus, yes we do.
We love Jesus, how about you?"
Back and forth the challenge
was batted like a tennis ball.
The early angelic smiles
soon became sneerful,
as each side wanted to win
the "Love Jesus" chant.
Voices became higher-pitched,
more shrill,
more unpleasant to hear
with increased volume.

Meanwhile, across town,
someone
silently
fed a hungry person.

Men Asking for Directions

Moses led the people forty long years
and his stubbornness brought them rejections.
They couldn't enter the Promised Land
because real men don't ask for directions.

Directions are found on all that we buy
for assembling with proper connections.
Men only read after messing it up
because real men don't ask for directions.

When continually getting lost as I drive,
with my wife shouting out her objections,
I tell her I'll find my way very soon
because real men don't ask for directions.

Life is not easy and all men get lost
as they turn at the wrong intersections.
My Bible gives the instructions I need
because real men do ask for directions.

Near Drowning

Spring fever was all around
as the lake welcomed our school
to the annual outing
with picnic,
boating,
and water skiing.

I was a the new kid on the block,
barely known by the rest,
who assumed that my swimsuit
announced my swimming ability
from the end of the dock.

With only a simple shove,
I found myself sinking below the surface
as the only person who knew
I could not swim.

Surfacing, my arms flailing,
a quick breath
and a return below the surface.
The second time up
was a clone of the first.
What if a boat would come by?

A classmate I hardly knew
became my closest friend
as he swam to my side
and dragged me to shore.

There are times in our lives
when we get in over our head
and bobble up and down
gasping for life.

We may feel the worst
will happen to us
as we kick ourselves up
from the bottom each time.

We survive until that friend
comes to our aid
and brings us new life
and helps plant our feet
on solid ground.

Poor Little Camp Girl

She came from a small country church to camp
although she couldn't afford to pay;
her church had paid for everything
plus some money for her to play.
In that same camp were girls of wealth
to whom money was only a toy,
and in the mix was one girl-hating boy.
The girls of wealth devised a fun scheme
when they went to canteen the next day.
"Let's all buy T-shirts that are made alike
and we'll all look exactly the same way."
The counselor spoke with wisdom and care:
"Maybe it's something not all can afford."
They never gave thought to the poor little girl
as they made their choice in one accord.
After swimming, they got candy and a Coke
and a beautiful T-shirt from camp,
while the poor girl stood alone back under a tree,
feeling the shame of a tramp.
The counselor said to the clerk in the shop,
"See that girl out under that tree?
When she comes in to get her a drink,
give her a T-shirt and don't say it's from me."
It may have been cloudy on that afternoon
but the clouds all left for a while
as that sweet little girl was given a shirt
and sunlight burst out through her smile.

Salty Christians

Jesus said you are the salt of the earth,
a candle shining as a leading light,
something to be highly desired,
leading struggling people through the night.

Lot's wife didn't fit this helpful image
she, too, was salt—so just what did she lack?
The answer is very simple, I'm sure:
She couldn't be helpful because she looked back.

Those who want to follow Jesus today
need to see if they are on the right track.
He needs those who are looking forward,
rather than those constantly looking back.

So don't tell me all the things that you have done,
but tell me what you're going to do.
If you explore where Jesus is going
the right kind of salt will be part of you.

The Old Camp Dog

He greets each camper every year
and tries to get you to scratch his ear.
He follows along where everyone goes
and gets so close, he steps on your toes.
The old camp dog.

There's one like him at every camp
who swims in the lake and comes back damp
or sometimes covered with old slimy matter
and shakes so you're all covered with splatter.
The old camp dog.

He may be called Shep or Buddy or Dude,
and as you eat, he watches for food
that drops to the ground right at your feet,
giving him something extra to eat.
The old camp dog.

He has more friends than most of us do.
When one group's leaving, another is due.
He must live in heaven—at least he's convinced
and there's no way he plans on budging an inch.
The old camp dog.

The Softball Sermon

"Would you like to know how," I asked one Sunday morn
As I was preaching to the crowd,
"to stay awake lying on the couch
while watching the Royals lose on TV?"

They hissed and booed and waved their hands
to show me they were displeased.
You see, I'm a Cardinal fan
in the midst of Royal country.

"Well," I asked, "do you want to know
or do you just want to sit and boo?"
They shouted, "Tell us,"
not knowing what I would say.

"It's simple," I told them,
"so let me tell you how.
Lying on the couch, cradle a softball in your hand.
You hold that softball in the air
as comfortably as you can.
When you go to sleep,
as the Royals make you do,
the ball will drop to the floor
and will awaken you."

A week later, my scripture was read
and my sermon was ready to go.
I opened my mouth and started to preach—
twenty softballs were cradled
as comfortably as they could.

The Un-traffic Jam

That unfriendly, nagging alarm clock went off
to remind me to go to the work I scoff.
Grumbling was the only way I could say
"I'm so tired of this drudgery every day."
Going through the motions of acting alert
as I put on yesterday's sweat-soaked shirt.
I combed my teeth and brushed my hair
And cut myself shaving, which caused me to swear.
I cannot remember just what I ate;
no time for the shower—it'll just have to wait.
As I drove down the street, I felt deep dismay
Where are all the cars we have every day?
Was my clock wrong? Did it go off too soon?
Was it six in the morning or six after noon?
But where's that rush-hour traffic I disdain
Which causes me tension and makes me insane?
Perhaps the "fundies" have always been right,
And the rapture occurred sometime last night.
Those crazy commuters who make my life hell
Have gone off to heaven and wished me farewell.
What must I do? Is it too late to pray?
To admit I was wrong is too hard to say.
Just a minute … the church lot is jammed
That means, thank God, I'm really not damned.
Now I know why the traffic was so thin—
People were at church, confessing their sin.
It's Sunday and I am not left in the lurch
Although I am sorry—I have just missed church.

Victim Redefined

It happens almost every day
as a wrong-doer gets up to say
"I was a victim of the press,"
and asks each of us to bless
the actions he was taking,
even though it was his own making.

This is hard for me to do
because of real victims I knew
who suffered through no choice of their own
and whose scars make them feel alone.

I've sat and cried with victims true
and felt, with them, their point of view.
I've seen them crippled for many years
and tried to deal with all their fears.

"Snap out of it," we preach to them
as we continue to condemn
the one abused and not the abuser
who, after all, is a real loser.

I, for one, mourn this trend
to those who try to defend
their poor choice that they make
and steal this word as a mistake.

Let's ask those who abuse this word
to cease from being so absurd.
Let's ask them to stand up and be strong
and simply say the words, "I was wrong!"

Who Touched Me?

"Who touched me?"
he asked that big crowd.
"Is it I?" the disciples asked in unison.
"Save that line for the Last Supper," Jesus replied.
"Of course you were touched;
it's a very big crowd."
"If I did it, I didn't mean to. I'm sorry!"
"I know I was touched because I felt my power being drained!"
It became very quiet as nobody spoke.
They looked in each other's faces.
She stumbled toward him
so feeble, so weak
and yet she seemed to glow like the sun.
She fell at his feet, prepared for a scolding.
She said, "I'm sorry, sweet Lord."
She told of twelve years of suffering so much
and she felt that she'd get well with a small touch.
A small touch!
I wonder as I sit here today
how many times has that touch of the Lord
been received in our very day.
Although he is not here in his body to serve,
could it be that the touch spreads today
when someone who loves and follows the Lord
brings a caring touch to one in need?

Take time to thank God before you go on
for the people from your past
who have touched your life and brought a good change.
Then, with the faith of that frail little woman,
ask Jesus to help your faith grow
so you too can be one who touches a very needy soul.
Who touched you?
Whose life will Jesus touch through you?
You may be surprised.

All-American Zoo

I went to the All-American Zoo today.
So many animals had gathered to play.
Wal-Mart was printed all over the place.
Action was running at a feverish pace.

As I entered, I saw some old people in blue.
They were so friendly and greeted me too.
The animals I met were all in such a rage.
I don't know when they escaped from their cage.

I saw a rhino where I wanted to go,
and he filled the aisle and traveled real slow.
In his hurry, the elephant lost his long list
but thanks to his memory, nothing was missed.

A pair of hyenas was parked in the aisle.
They stood with each other and laughed for a while.
A giraffe had an advantage that wasn't for me.
The things on the top shelf were easy to see.

Some of the animals had all of their young.
When I got to a corner, out one of them sprung.
In fear, I started to run from the door
and would you believe, there were two more?

It said it was Wal-Mart, but it must be a zoo.
There were monkeys and apes and gorillas, too.
I quickly checked out from this supermarket.
I wonder how different it would be at Target.

From Shadows to Spotlight

She was a shadow-dweller.
Her father was a pastor
and she shadowed him
and supported him.

Her plans to be a missionary
took the back seat
and she married a young pastor
and supported him.

Through the years, she sat in the shadows
and smiled as her husband served.
There she sat in the shade
and supported him.

She had three children
who accomplished many things.
She sat in their shadows
and supported them.

Her day came, as it always does
for those who serve others.
And she made a name for herself,
standing in the spotlight of the sun.

Today they honored her
with talks and gifts and such.
And her husband stood proudly in the shadows
and supported her.

God's Love at the Restaurant

They sat and ate so quietly.
No word did they share.
They ate silently
in a restaurant crowd right there.
I sat across the room
and fought back salty tears.
I remembered times not long ago
not so many years.
Their talking would not cease
as they told their tales together.
One would start the story
And it was finished by the other.
And a person sat there listening
with no chance to say a word.
Then everyone would laugh
at the story that they heard.

Illness came to visit
as an enemy from hell.
He hears and sees and understands
but the words he cannot tell.
His body is strong
and you cannot tell he's ill.
The caring love of his partner
gives my heart a chill.

I spoke to them as they left.
Both of them smiled at me.
I watched them going out the door
as far as I could see.
Then, with my folded napkin,
I dabbed at a tear or two
to see God's love in action
and knowing how it grew.
And I remembered the good times.

If Isaiah Was Alive Today
(based on Isaiah 1:10-20)

If Isaiah was alive today,
would he approve of the way we pray?
Our beautiful sanctuaries—He's not impressed
and He's hardly excited at the way we are dressed.
Traditional hymns and organs don't take the cake
and our long-winded sermons can't keep Him awake.
Our cute little promotions—don't get me wrong
are far too distracting—He can't hear our song.
He doesn't see the things we think are so cool,
while our treatment of others is so very cruel.
He turns off the music that comes from our bands
because of the bloodstain He sees on our hands.
We don't hear Him ask us, "Where are the poor?"
We think He is saying, "Please lock the door."
What if He appeared as a guest we should warmly greet,
and our first words to Him are, "Please move, that's my seat!"
Now, before you miss my big point
and begin to get your nose out of joint,
it may not be that He's not listening to you
when your actions don't follow the things He would do.
More likely, my friend, I must make it clear
our unloving actions make it so we can't hear.
Since worship truly is a two-way street
the way we treat neighbors makes it complete.
The good and obedient shall be fully fed
and our worship will boldly rise from the dead.

Loudness or Silence

Loudness or silence,
which do I choose?
Which do I keep
and which do I lose?

"Make a joyful noise …"
"Be still and know …"
practice your faith—
but don't let it show.

Bi-polar spirituality
is our plight.
We are so divided;
are we ever right?

Jesus was able to combine
both practices in His life.
He benefited from what
could have brought Him strife.

We can try to follow
the example He gave.
Employing His direction
as we learn how to behave.

The question isn't
which one comes first.
It's a blessed circle
that can't be rehearsed.

Each leads to the other,
moving us higher,
increasing, improving
our spiritual fire.

My Addiction

I'm addicted, and I'm so glad
because this addiction's not so bad.
I know it is really taxing on me,
but it is something that makes me free.

It reaches deep into my pocketbook,
steals as efficiently as any crook.
Sometimes it causes me to lose much rest
and can put my stamina to the test.

Embarrassment pops up once in a while
and leaves me showing a silly-faced smile,
whene'er I say something wrong to someone
and feel like I should turn around and run.

My addiction is people, you see.
I touch their lives and in turn, they touch me.
All people are the greatest reason why.
That they do give me a natural high.

Old Country House

Out in the middle of the countryside
is a house where families used to reside.
The swayback roof once was so tough—
now the bad wolf would not need to huff
and puff to blow it down,
since everyone has moved to town.

Think of the stories it could tell
when families were there and all was well.
It was built with such a plain décor
and now it's missing every door
that let in all the cats and dogs
and once or twice some errant hogs.
The screen that once kept out the flies
and filtered the aroma of fresh-baked pies
is rusted and hanging from the wall,
ready with the softest breeze, to fall.

That big front porch holds a fallen limb
that's big and broken and kind of slim.
Some missing steps that once were sound
lie under the porch upon the ground
Remembering the children's hungry drool
as they ran for snacks right after school.

A tire at the end of a rotting rope
hangs from a limb with a gentle slope
longing for the little child
who sat in it for hours and smiled
as a parent gave the tire a shove—
a little task that was done with love.

What stories remain in this lonely place
when life was lived at a rapid pace—
Christmas, Thanksgiving stories to tell
and big birthday parties as well.
If that house spoke and we all could hear,
do you think we'd shed many a tear
at the treasures that rickety building can hold
of much more value than silver or gold?

Rock Concerts and Jesus

The concert season is in full swing.
The big-name idols are there to sing.
The tickets cost more than I can afford.
That's one more thing to be ignored.

People come from points far away
to watch these people sing and play.
They'll use plastic to cover the price,
and go into debt and not think twice.

If Jesus appeared in a coliseum,
I wonder how many would go to see him.
Would the same people crowd in there?
Or would they think that he's too square?

This question we really shouldn't pursue.
The real decision is—what would you do?
Would you stay at home because of the cost,
Or go in search of those who are "lost?"

His method is not to stand and perform.
He wants to help us as we reform.
He wants us to remove all our tethers,
And bring his kind of love to others.

Saved From or Saved For

"Are you saved?" they ask in a confronting voice.
"Will you go to heaven when you die?"
Why are they obsessed with these questions
and do nothing to help people live now?
We can answer all their questions
and get baptized with the proper wetness
and put our names on the "books."
But we can still be just as dead in our heart.

What do they believe about this life we live today?
Does living only come to us when we die?
Don't they think that God loves it
when we do our living now?
Feeding the hungry and helping the sick—
clothing the naked and hearing those who are alone—
washing the feet and giving cold water.
Being a servant—like Jesus was.

Could they help us so much more
by surrounding us with life?
And replace all their judging
with the gift of caring love.
The kind of love Jesus showed us
when he walked upon this earth.
Then we will live with fullness
in the days before our death.

Spider's Frightening Ride

On a quiet summer night under a star
he carefully climbed the nearest parked car
to find a place to spin his delicate bed
so he'd have a place to lay his head.
There were many good choices on that car;
he spotted one from afar
from the driver's door to the side-view mirror,
he knew his web would adhere.
Seemed like the most perfect place
to hang his silk hammock in space.
Morning arrived with a violent shock
as the driver slammed the door.
The old silk bed began to rock
but there was soon to be much more.
As the car drove away, the web slowly shook
like a very small earthquake
in a gentle vibration that told him
there were precautions he needed to take.
With the car achieving freeway speed,
if he was a dog he would bark.

The web became like a ride, indeed,
at the nearby amusement park
on all the rides in the entire site
as he clung on with all his might.
With no hand-lifting and shouting with glee,
instead he shouted his spider yell—"Help me."
Back and forth and up and down
on this nonstop drive all over town.
Those webs are strong, or so I am told,
but at sixty-five, the web didn't hold.
It wasn't with the greatest of grace
that his evening's bed was thrown into space.
I don't know what happened as the web came undone
and he flew in the air in the web he had spun.
If he survived, and I pray that he did,
I'm sure his emotions didn't stay hid.
Think of the story he had to share
About this ultimate ride in the air.

Strangers from the Past

I've moved around a lot.
Many people have I known.
I am like a gardener
after many seeds are sown.

No matter where I seem to be
I often am aghast;
when I least expect it,
there's someone from my past.

Sometimes it's someone I have known
whose name I can't recall,
when eating at a restaurant
or shopping at a mall.

I visit with a stranger
who is completely new.
We find they know someone
and I have known them too.

When we share our lives with folks
as we live upon this earth,
God will take those experiences
and give them added worth.

This happened just the other night
when I made a hospital call.
One I thought would be a stranger
was an acquaintance after all.

The American Idol

Millions of people watch every week the *American Idol* show.
They miss other things so they can help to decide
who will stay or will go.
One by one, the contestants go home, till only one person is there.
They are given a title which they do not have to share.

I wonder who the real American Idols are.
A father who works many hours
to provide for his family's need.
A teacher who gives up lucrative pay
to help our youth succeed.
The cop on the corner, the firefighter on call,
the soldier who leaves our fair land.
A Christian who sings in the choir
and another who plays in the band.
A social worker giving a helping hand
a missionary working in a foreign land.

These folks won't make millions
but their pay will be more.
They continue their service even though they are sore.
The bonus is given to those with the nerve
whose ultimate goal is to reach out and serve.

It is more blessed to give than to receive
the man from Nazareth said.
You learn the value of his excellent words
when you are Spirit-led
And forget the praise and just do what you can.
Then, and only then, my friend
you are a true American Idol,
whether you're a woman or a man.

Under New Management

The old store stood there idle,
abandoned in a lifeless shell.
The fact that it once jumped with action
was impossible to tell.
A flurry of activity
suddenly filled the air.
Now a big bright banner hangs
like a fiery roadside flare.
Things will be different somehow—
it's under new management now.

The season has gone from bad to worse
for the local baseball team.
Prospects that once looked so bright
have become a most painful dream.
They've traded players with no success;
their record gets even worse.
Some even thought they'd been hit
by some superstitious curse.
The skipper took his final bow—
They're under new management.

With life a mess and hope all gone
a messed-up man entered the door
of the small but beautiful church
where he'd never gone before.
Hymns were sung and prayers were prayed,
the preacher had something good to say.
It all mixed in a perfect blend;
God touched him in a special way.
He left that church with a brand new vow—
he's under new management now.

Printed in the United States
109742LV00002B/1-99/P

9 781434 365132